Social Impact of Mobile Phones in the Digital Age

C. P. Kumar
Reiki Healer
Roorkee - 247667, India

Disclaimer

While every effort has been made to ensure the accuracy and completeness of the content in this book, the author cannot guarantee that the information contained herein is error-free, up-to-date, or suitable for every individual circumstance.

The author shall not be held liable or responsible for any errors or omissions in the content of the book, nor for any damages, or losses that may arise from any actions taken based upon the suggestions or contents presented in the book.

Readers are advised to use their own judgment and discretion in applying the information provided in this book, and to consult with qualified professionals before taking any action based on the contents of this book. The author disclaims any and all liability or responsibility for any actions taken or not taken based on the information contained in this book.

DEDICATION

To all those who have explored the profound impact of mobile phones in our digital age,

This book is dedicated to you.

From breaking geographical barriers to redefining relationships, from shaping identity to fostering community, mobile phones have reshaped our social landscape. Through the chapters that follow, we delve into the intricate ways in which these devices have influenced our lives.

May this book inspire reflection, spark conversations, and propel us towards a future where mobile technology serves as a catalyst for positive social change.

With gratitude and anticipation,

C. P. Kumar

CONTENTS

Copyright...2

Disclaimer...3

DEDICATION...4

PREFACE..7

Chapter 1.   The Mobile Revolution and Its Social
Consequences 9

Chapter 2.   The Evolution of Communication 13

Chapter 3.   Mobile Phones and Social Connectivity.............16

Chapter 4.   The Rise of Social Media 20

Chapter 5.   Shaping Identity 25

Chapter 6.   Social Networking and Community Building......28

Chapter 7.   Mobile Phones and Family Dynamics 32

Chapter 8.   Love and Romance in the Digital Era 36

Chapter 9.   Cyberbullying and Online Harassment..............40

Chapter 10.   Privacy and Surveillance 44

Chapter 11.   Mobile Phones and Mental Health....................48

Chapter 12.   Education and Learning 52

Chapter 13.   Work-Life Balance in the Digital Age 56

Chapter 14.   Civic Engagement and Activism.........................60

Chapter 15. Mobile Phones and Intergenerational Relationships...64

Chapter 16. The Future of Mobile Technology 67

PREFACE

In the digital age, mobile phones have transformed the way we communicate, connect, and navigate our social landscape. This book delves into the social impact of mobile phones in the digital era, examining their influence on various aspects of our lives and relationships.

The chapters in this book explore the multifaceted consequences of the mobile revolution. We begin by introducing the profound changes brought about by mobile technology and its pervasive influence on society. From there, we delve into the evolution of communication, from traditional face-to-face interactions to the virtual connections facilitated by mobile phones. We then explore the role of mobile phones in breaking geographical barriers, allowing individuals to connect and communicate across distances.

The rise of social media is examined, with a focus on how it has redefined relationships and social norms in the digital age. We also investigate the impact of mobile phones on shaping identity and self-presentation.

The power of online platforms for social networking and community building is explored, along with their implications for personal and collective connections. Mobile phones' influence on family dynamics is examined, including how they can bridge or strain bonds within families. Love and romance in the digital era are addressed, with a specific focus on the role of mobile dating apps and their impact on relationship formation. The darker side of connectivity is also explored, examining the issues of cyberbullying and online harassment.

The book further delves into the delicate balance between privacy and surveillance in the age of mobile technology. We investigate the impact of constant connectivity on mental health and well-being, as well as the potential of mobile phones as tools for education and knowledge access.

Work-life balance in the digital age is examined, considering the challenges of maintaining professional boundaries in an always-connected world. The book then explores the transformative power of mobile phones for civic engagement and activism, as well as their role in bridging intergenerational gaps. Finally, we take a glimpse into the future, anticipating the social shifts that mobile technology will continue to bring about in a connected world.

By exploring these various dimensions, this book aims to provide readers with a comprehensive understanding of the social impact of mobile phones in the digital age. It highlights the opportunities, challenges, and complexities inherent in our increasingly connected world, empowering readers to navigate the evolving digital landscape with greater awareness and insight.

C. P. Kumar
Reiki Healer
Former Scientist 'G', National Institute of Hydrology
Roorkee - 247667, India
E-mail: cpkumar@yahoo.com
Web: https://www.angelfire.com/nh/cpkumar/virgo.html

Chapter 1. The Mobile Revolution and Its Social Consequences

Introduction

The advent of mobile technology has ushered in a remarkable revolution that has transformed the way we live, work, and interact with one another. Over the past few decades, mobile devices have become an integral part of our daily lives, connecting us to a vast world of information, communication, and entertainment. This article explores the social consequences of the mobile revolution, highlighting both its positive and negative impacts on society.

Enhanced Connectivity

The mobile revolution has brought about unprecedented levels of connectivity, allowing people to stay connected with each other regardless of their physical location. Mobile devices enable real-time communication through voice calls, text messages, and instant messaging applications. This connectivity has bridged the gap between people and has made it easier to maintain relationships, both personal and professional. Friends and family can now stay in touch effortlessly, even if they are separated by great distances. Additionally, businesses have benefited from increased connectivity, as employees can collaborate seamlessly regardless of their physical location.

Access to Information

One of the most significant social consequences of the mobile revolution is the democratization of information.

Mobile devices provide instant access to a vast amount of information through the internet. People can now search for information, news, and resources on-the-go, empowering them with knowledge like never before. This has had a profound impact on education, as students can access online courses, tutorials, and educational materials anytime, anywhere. The availability of information has also contributed to a more informed and aware society, enabling individuals to make better decisions and stay updated on global events.

Social Media and Connectivity

The rise of social media platforms has been closely intertwined with the mobile revolution, shaping the way we interact and share our lives with others. Platforms like Facebook, Instagram, and Twitter have become virtual communities, connecting people from all walks of life. Social media has given individuals a platform to express their opinions, share experiences, and build communities around shared interests. However, it has also brought about certain challenges, such as the rise of online harassment, cyberbullying, and the spread of misinformation. The impact of social media on mental health has also been a subject of concern, with studies highlighting the negative effects of excessive social media use.

Changing Work Patterns

The mobile revolution has disrupted traditional work patterns, giving rise to remote work and flexible schedules. Mobile devices and internet connectivity have enabled employees to work from anywhere, reducing the need for a fixed physical office space. This has led to increased work-life balance, as individuals can manage their professional responsibilities while having more flexibility in their personal lives. However, this shift has also blurred the boundaries between work and personal life, leading to challenges such as burnout and difficulty in disconnecting from work obligations.

Impact on Physical and Mental Health

While the mobile revolution has undoubtedly brought numerous benefits, it has also raised concerns about its impact on physical and mental health. Excessive screen time and sedentary lifestyles associated with mobile device usage have contributed to a rise in health issues such as obesity, eye strain, and musculoskeletal problems. Moreover, the constant connectivity and information overload can lead to heightened stress levels and a decreased ability to focus. It is crucial for individuals to find a balance in their mobile device usage and prioritize their well-being.

Privacy and Security Concerns

With the increasing reliance on mobile devices for personal and professional purposes, privacy and security concerns have come to the forefront. The collection and storage of personal data by mobile applications and service providers raise questions about data privacy and potential misuse. Instances of data breaches and unauthorized access to personal information have highlighted the need for robust security measures to protect users' privacy. Society must address these concerns and ensure that individuals have control over their personal data and are well-informed about privacy settings and security practices.

Conclusion

The mobile revolution has brought about a seismic shift in society, transforming the way we connect, access information, work, and engage with the world. While the benefits of enhanced connectivity, access to information, and flexible work patterns are undeniable, it is crucial to address the challenges posed by excessive screen time, mental health issues, and privacy concerns. As we navigate the mobile era, it is essential to strike a balance between leveraging the positive aspects of mobile technology while mitigating its negative social consequences. By doing so, we can ensure that the mobile revolution continues to empower individuals and enhance our lives while promoting a healthy and secure digital society.

Chapter 2. The Evolution of Communication
From Face-to-Face to Virtual Connections

Introduction

In today's digital age, the way we communicate with one another has undergone a remarkable transformation. With the advent of mobile phones and the rise of virtual connections, traditional face-to-face interactions have given way to a new era of communication. This article explores the evolution of communication, tracing its journey from personal encounters to the virtual realm, and examines the social impact of mobile phones in shaping our interconnected world.

The Era of Face-to-Face Communication

Throughout history, face-to-face communication has been the cornerstone of human interaction. From ancient civilizations to modern societies, people have relied on direct personal encounters to convey thoughts, emotions, and ideas. Face-to-face communication allowed for nuanced expression, non-verbal cues, and real-time feedback, fostering deep connections and building social bonds. However, this mode of communication was limited by distance, time, and the need for physical presence.

The Dawn of Telecommunication

The invention of the telegraph in the 19th century revolutionized long-distance communication. It enabled people to exchange messages across vast distances, transcending geographical barriers. Later, the telephone further transformed communication by allowing real-time voice conversations, bridging the gap between individuals separated by miles. While these advancements facilitated remote communication, they still required individuals to be present at designated locations to send or receive messages.

Mobile Phones: The Birth of Mobility

The advent of mobile phones marked a significant turning point in communication. With the ability to carry devices on the go, individuals were no longer bound to a specific location to connect with others. Mobile phones introduced unprecedented mobility, enabling people to communicate from virtually anywhere. This newfound freedom brought convenience and efficiency, allowing for immediate communication and breaking down the constraints of distance.

The Rise of Virtual Connections

As technology progressed, so did the ways we connect with one another. The emergence of the internet and the proliferation of smartphones paved the way for virtual connections. Social media platforms, instant messaging apps, and video conferencing tools became integral parts of our daily lives, transforming how we interact with others. These virtual connections transcended physical barriers, facilitating communication with individuals across the globe. People could now engage in real-time conversations, share information, and maintain relationships irrespective of distance.

Social Impact of Mobile Phones

The rise of mobile phones and virtual connections has had a profound social impact. On one hand, it has brought people closer, fostering global communities and breaking down cultural boundaries. Individuals can now connect with friends, family, and colleagues instantly, regardless of their physical location. Moreover, social media platforms have enabled the sharing of ideas, experiences, and perspectives on a global scale, empowering individuals to find like-minded communities and drive social change.

However, the constant presence of mobile phones and virtual connections has also presented challenges. The addictive nature of smartphones and the allure of social media have led to concerns about privacy, mental health, and the erosion of face-to-face interactions. The need for constant connectivity can create a sense of isolation, as individuals prioritize virtual relationships over real-world connections. It is crucial to strike a balance and use technology as a tool to enhance communication while maintaining meaningful personal interactions.

Conclusion

The evolution of communication from face-to-face encounters to virtual connections has shaped the way we interact in the digital age. Mobile phones have revolutionized communication by enabling mobility and breaking down physical barriers. While virtual connections offer unparalleled convenience and connectivity, it is important to remember the value of face-to-face interactions. Technology should enhance, rather than replace, personal connections. As we navigate this rapidly changing landscape, we must strive for a harmonious integration of traditional and virtual communication methods, ensuring that technology serves as a bridge, not a barrier, to human connection.

Introduction

In the modern era, mobile phones have become an indispensable part of our lives. They have revolutionized the way we communicate, bridging geographical barriers and connecting people from all corners of the globe. With the advancement of technology, mobile phones have evolved into powerful devices that not only facilitate voice calls but also enable us to stay socially connected through various applications and platforms. In this article, we will explore how mobile phones have transformed social connectivity, transcending physical boundaries and bringing people together like never before.

Mobile Phones: A Global Communication Tool

Mobile phones have truly transformed communication by making it easier, faster, and more convenient. With just a few taps on a screen, we can connect with friends, family, and colleagues, regardless of their location. The advent of smartphones and mobile applications has provided us with a plethora of options to stay connected, such as voice calls, text messaging, video calls, and social media platforms.

Social Media: Connecting People Worldwide

One of the most significant contributions of mobile phones to social connectivity is the rise of social media platforms. These platforms, such as Facebook, Twitter, Instagram, and Snapchat, have enabled people to connect, share experiences, and form communities beyond geographical boundaries. Social media platforms have become virtual meeting places where individuals can interact with people they might never have met otherwise. Whether it's reuniting with old friends, staying in touch with family abroad, or making new connections, social media has revolutionized the way we build and maintain relationships.

Instant Messaging: Real-Time Communication

The rise of instant messaging applications, such as WhatsApp, Messenger, and WeChat, has further enhanced social connectivity. These applications allow us to send text messages, voice notes, images, and even make voice and video calls, all in real-time. With instant messaging, geographical barriers become insignificant, as we can engage in conversations with people across different time zones instantly. Whether it's coordinating plans with friends, collaborating on projects with colleagues, or simply catching up with loved ones, instant messaging has made communication effortless and seamless.

Video Calling: Face-to-Face Connections

Mobile phones have also brought face-to-face interactions to a whole new level with the introduction of video calling. Applications like Skype, FaceTime, and Google Meet enable us to have virtual meetings, conduct interviews, or simply have a heartfelt conversation with our loved ones, regardless of the distance between us. Video calling adds a personal touch to communication, as we can see facial expressions and body language, fostering a sense of connection that traditional voice calls cannot replicate.

Mobile Apps: Connecting Communities

Mobile applications have opened up a world of possibilities when it comes to connecting communities. From dating apps that connect potential partners based on interests and preferences to language exchange apps that allow people to learn new languages and engage with native speakers, mobile apps have broken down barriers and facilitated meaningful connections between individuals with shared interests or goals. These apps have created virtual spaces where people can find like-minded individuals and build relationships beyond geographical limitations.

Impact on Business and Networking

Mobile phones have also had a profound impact on business and networking. Through professional networking platforms like LinkedIn, individuals can connect with industry peers, expand their professional network, and explore new career opportunities, regardless of their physical location. Mobile phones have made it possible to attend virtual conferences, webinars, and workshops, allowing professionals to gain knowledge, share ideas, and collaborate with experts from around the world.

Conclusion

Mobile phones have undeniably revolutionized social connectivity by breaking geographical barriers. Through social media, instant messaging, video calling, and mobile applications, we can connect with people globally, fostering relationships, and expanding our horizons. The ability to communicate and engage with others, irrespective of their location, has transformed the way we live, work, and interact. As mobile technology continues to advance, we can expect even greater connectivity, bringing people closer together and making the world a smaller, more connected place.

Chapter 4. The Rise of Social Media
Redefining Relationships in the Digital Age

Introduction

In the digital age, the rise of social media platforms has transformed the way we connect, communicate, and build relationships. Mobile phones, coupled with the power of social media, have created a global network that transcends geographical boundaries, fostering new opportunities and challenges for individuals and society as a whole. This article explores the social impact of mobile phones and social media platforms, delving into how they have redefined relationships in the digital age.

The Digital Revolution and Connectivity

The advent of mobile phones and social media has revolutionized connectivity, allowing people to communicate instantaneously regardless of their physical location. Long gone are the days when distance served as a barrier to maintaining relationships. With a few taps on a screen, we can now connect with friends, family, and even strangers from across the globe. Social media platforms have become virtual meeting places, where individuals can share their thoughts, photos, and experiences, fostering a sense of interconnectedness and community.

The Evolution of Social Interaction

Social media has redefined the way we interact with one another. Traditional forms of communication, such as face-to-face conversations and phone calls, have taken a backseat to instant messaging and social media updates. These platforms offer a sense of convenience, enabling individuals to communicate at their own pace and on their terms. However, this shift has also raised concerns about the quality and depth of our interactions. While social media provides a platform for quick exchanges, it may lack the nuance and emotional depth that personal interactions offer.

Building and Maintaining Relationships

Social media platforms have become instrumental in building and maintaining relationships. They provide a space for individuals to showcase their lives, interests, and achievements, allowing others to stay connected and engaged. Moreover, social media facilitates the discovery of new relationships, connecting people with shared interests or common causes. From long-lost friends to potential romantic partners, social media has expanded our options for forging connections. However, it is important to strike a balance between virtual and real-world relationships, as online interactions can sometimes fall short of the richness found in face-to-face connections.

The Influence of Social Media on Self-Identity

Social media platforms have also reshaped the way we construct our self-identity. Users curate their online personas, carefully selecting what they share with the world. This curation can influence how others perceive them and how they perceive themselves. While social media allows for self-expression and empowerment, it can also breed comparison and self-esteem issues. The pressure to present an idealized version of oneself can lead to feelings of inadequacy and a distorted sense of reality.

Popular Social Media Platforms

The rise of social media has given birth to numerous platforms that have garnered millillions, and in some cases billions, of active users. Here are a few of the most popular social media platforms that have had a significant impact on the digital landscape:

Facebook: Launched in 2004, Facebook has become the largest social media platform, boasting over 2.989 billion monthly active users as of April 2023. It offers a wide range of features, including personalized user profiles, news feeds, photo and video sharing, and groups. Facebook has become a virtual hub for connecting with friends, family, and colleagues, as well as a platform for sharing news and engaging with various communities and organizations.

Instagram: Initially introduced as a photo-sharing platform in 2010, Instagram quickly gained popularity and was acquired by Facebook in 2012. It has since evolved into a full-fledged social media platform, with over 1 billion active users. Instagram focuses on visual content, allowing users to share photos and videos, apply filters and effects, and engage with others through likes, comments, and direct messages. It has become particularly popular among younger demographics and influencers.

Twitter: Known for its unique format of short-form messages called tweets, Twitter has played a significant role in shaping online conversations and real-time news sharing. With approximately 353 million monthly active users in 2023, Twitter has become a go-to platform for sharing thoughts, opinions, and news updates in a concise manner. Its use of hashtags has made it a powerful tool for organizing discussions around specific topics and events.

LinkedIn: While other social media platforms focus on personal connections, LinkedIn is designed primarily for professional networking and career development. With 922 million members in April 2023, LinkedIn allows individuals to showcase their professional skills, work experience, and achievements. It facilitates connections with colleagues, industry professionals, and potential employers, making it a valuable platform for job seekers, recruiters, and professionals looking to expand their networks.

These are just a few examples of the diverse social media platforms that have reshaped the way we connect and interact with others in the digital age. Each platform offers its unique features and appeals to different audiences, reflecting the evolving landscape of social media in the modern world.

The Impact on Social Activism

Social media has emerged as a powerful tool for social activism and raising awareness. Movements and causes can now gain momentum rapidly, as information spreads like wildfire through digital networks. Hashtags, viral campaigns, and online petitions have become commonplace in driving social change. The ease and accessibility of social media make it a platform for marginalized voices to be heard, providing a means to challenge established norms and advocate for justice.

Privacy and Security Concerns

As social media continues to penetrate every aspect of our lives, privacy and security concerns have arisen. Users must grapple with the trade-off between sharing personal information and safeguarding their privacy. Instances of data breaches, online harassment, and identity theft have highlighted the need for robust security measures and responsible digital citizenship. Balancing the benefits of social media with the protection of personal information is a critical challenge in the digital age.

Conclusion

The rise of social media, propelled by the ubiquity of mobile phones, has undoubtedly redefined relationships in the digital age. It has revolutionized connectivity, transformed social interaction, and influenced self-identity. While offering immense opportunities for building relationships and driving social change, social media also presents challenges in terms of depth of interaction, privacy, and security. As we navigate the digital landscape, it is crucial to be mindful of the impact of social media on our relationships and to strike a balance between the virtual and the real. Only then can we harness the full potential of social media while safeguarding the authenticity and depth of our connections in the ever-evolving digital age.

Chapter 5. Shaping Identity
The Role of Mobile Phones in Self-Presentation

Introduction

In the modern era, mobile phones have become an indispensable part of our lives. These devices are no longer mere communication tools but have transformed into extensions of our identities. With the advent of smartphones and their powerful features, we have gained the ability to present ourselves to the world in new and diverse ways. This article explores the significant role mobile phones play in shaping our identities through self-presentation, highlighting the impact they have on various aspects of our lives.

The Power of Visual Storytelling

In today's digital age, mobile phones have become a hub for visual storytelling. With high-quality cameras and numerous photo editing applications, individuals can capture and share moments that reflect their personal narratives. From carefully curated Instagram feeds to Snapchat stories and TikTok videos, mobile phones enable users to craft a visual representation of themselves that aligns with their desired self-image.

Social Media and Personal Branding

Social media platforms have revolutionized the way we present ourselves to others. Mobile phones serve as portals to these platforms, allowing us to curate and showcase our lives through carefully selected posts and profiles. We consciously create and maintain our personal brand, shaping how others perceive us. From LinkedIn for professional networking to Instagram for showcasing lifestyles, mobile phones have become essential tools for self-promotion and identity management.

Constant Connectivity and Online Persona

Mobile phones have transformed the way we connect with others, enabling us to be constantly available and engaged. Through messaging apps and social media platforms, we maintain an online presence that contributes to our digital identity. We carefully curate our online personas, projecting certain qualities, interests, and activities to align with our desired image. The mobile phone acts as a gateway, allowing us to shape our identities even in virtual spaces.

Fashion and Personal Style

The accessibility of mobile phones has had a profound impact on fashion and personal style. With fashion-forward applications and online shopping platforms at our fingertips, we can explore new trends, seek inspiration, and create unique looks. Mobile phones have become fashion companions, empowering individuals to experiment with different styles, curate fashion profiles, and seek validation from online communities. They play a pivotal role in shaping our sartorial identities and influencing our self-expression through clothing and accessories.

Empowerment and Self-Expression

Mobile phones have given a voice to those who may have otherwise been marginalized. Social media platforms and content creation tools enable individuals to express their perspectives, share their stories, and engage with diverse communities. People from all walks of life can now find spaces where they feel seen, heard, and validated. Mobile phones have played a crucial role in empowering individuals to embrace their identities and foster connections with like-minded individuals across the globe.

Privacy and the Illusion of Control

While mobile phones offer unprecedented opportunities for self-presentation, they also raise concerns regarding privacy and the illusion of control over our digital identities. With each photo shared, comment posted, or location tagged, we leave digital footprints that can be traced back to us. Mobile phones have blurred the line between private and public spaces, making it vital to consider the implications of the information we share and the long-term impact it may have on our identities.

Conclusion

Mobile phones have become essential tools for self-presentation, enabling us to shape and project our identities in ways never before possible. From visual storytelling to personal branding and online connectivity, these devices play a significant role in how we perceive ourselves and how others perceive us. However, it is important to remember that while mobile phones offer immense opportunities for self-expression, they also come with responsibilities and potential consequences. Striking a balance between authenticity and privacy is crucial as we navigate the ever-evolving landscape of digital identity in the age of mobile phones.

Introduction

In today's digital age, mobile phones have become an integral part of our lives, transforming the way we connect, communicate, and build relationships. One of the most profound impacts of mobile phones is the emergence of social networking platforms, which have revolutionized the concept of community building. These online platforms provide opportunities for individuals to connect, share, and collaborate, fostering a sense of belonging and empowering communities like never before. In this article, we will explore the power of social networking in community building, highlighting its positive impact on society.

The Rise of Online Social Networking

The advent of social networking platforms, such as Facebook, Twitter, and Instagram, has completely reshaped the way people interact and build relationships. These platforms offer individuals the ability to connect with friends, family, and even strangers across geographical boundaries. The ease of access provided by mobile phones has made social networking more accessible and pervasive than ever before, leading to a rapid increase in their popularity.

Creating Virtual Communities

Social networking platforms provide users with the ability to create and join virtual communities based on shared interests, hobbies, or causes. These communities act as gathering places for like-minded individuals to come together, exchange ideas, and form meaningful connections. Whether it's a group of photography enthusiasts, a support group for individuals dealing with mental health issues, or a network of professionals in a specific industry, online platforms enable the formation of communities that might not have been possible otherwise.

Facilitating Knowledge Sharing and Learning

One of the significant advantages of online social networking platforms is their ability to facilitate knowledge sharing and learning within communities. Through discussion forums, groups, and live chats, individuals can share their expertise, seek advice, and learn from others. This democratization of knowledge has empowered individuals from all walks of life to access information, skills, and resources that were once limited to a privileged few. Social networking platforms have become hubs of collective intelligence, promoting continuous learning and personal growth.

Amplifying Social Causes and Activism

Online platforms have emerged as powerful tools for raising awareness and mobilizing support for social causes and activism. Through social networking, individuals can share information, stories, and initiatives related to various social issues, amplifying their impact on a global scale. Whether it's fundraising for a charitable organization, organizing protests, or advocating for policy change, social networking has given individuals a platform to voice their concerns and rally support for meaningful change.

Building Support Networks

For individuals facing challenging circumstances or belonging to marginalized communities, social networking platforms can provide a lifeline of support and understanding. Online communities focused on mental health, chronic illnesses, LGBTQ+ rights, and other similar topics offer spaces where individuals can share their experiences, find empathy, and connect with others who face similar challenges. These support networks can play a vital role in combating isolation, promoting mental well-being, and fostering a sense of belonging.

Economic Empowerment and Entrepreneurship

Social networking platforms have also opened up new avenues for economic empowerment and entrepreneurship. Through these platforms, individuals can showcase their talents, products, and services to a global audience, eliminating traditional barriers to entry. Many small businesses and independent creators have found success by leveraging the power of online communities and social networking. These platforms provide a level playing field for aspiring entrepreneurs, allowing them to reach customers, collaborate with peers, and grow their businesses.

Overcoming Geographic Boundaries

One of the most remarkable aspects of social networking platforms is their ability to transcend geographical boundaries. Through these platforms, individuals can connect with people from different cultures, countries, and backgrounds, fostering cross-cultural understanding and global collaborations. This interconnectedness has the potential to break down barriers, promote empathy, and build bridges between communities that may have previously been isolated from one another.

Conclusion

In the digital age, social networking platforms have transformed the way we connect, communicate, and build communities. These online platforms have empowered individuals to create virtual communities, facilitate knowledge sharing, amplify social causes, build support networks, promote economic empowerment, and overcome geographic boundaries. While there are challenges and risks associated with social networking, it is undeniable that when harnessed responsibly, these platforms have the power to create a positive social impact. As we continue to navigate the digital landscape, understanding and harnessing the potential of online platforms in community building will be crucial for fostering a more connected and inclusive society.

Chapter 7. Mobile Phones and Family Dynamics
Bridging or Straining Bonds?

Introduction

In this digital age, mobile phones have become an integral part of our daily lives. They have revolutionized the way we communicate, work, and stay connected with our loved ones. However, the increasing use of mobile phones within families has raised questions about the impact on family dynamics. Are mobile phones bridging the gaps between family members or straining the bonds that hold them together? This article explores the various ways mobile phones can influence family relationships and the steps that can be taken to strike a healthy balance.

Connectivity and Communication

Mobile phones have undoubtedly enhanced connectivity and communication within families. With instant messaging apps, video calls, and social media platforms, family members can stay connected regardless of distance. Grandparents can witness their grandchildren's milestones in real time, and siblings can share their everyday experiences with one another. Mobile phones facilitate easy and convenient communication, making it easier for families to bridge the gap created by physical separation.

Disruption of Quality Time

While mobile phones enable constant communication, they can also disrupt the quality time that families spend together. In today's fast-paced world, it is common to see family members engrossed in their phones during meals or family gatherings, instead of engaging in meaningful conversations. This constant distraction can strain bonds and create a sense of disconnection among family members. It is crucial to establish boundaries and allocate specific times for phone usage to ensure that quality time is not compromised.

Social Media and the Pressure to Present a Perfect Image

Social media platforms have become a significant part of many people's lives, including families. While they can serve as a platform for sharing and connecting, they also create a pressure to present a perfect image of family life. The desire to curate an ideal online persona can strain family bonds as it may lead to unrealistic expectations and comparisons. It is important to promote open and honest conversations within the family and remind everyone that imperfections are normal and should be embraced.

Parent-Child Relationships

Mobile phones have a profound impact on parent-child relationships. On one hand, smartphones provide parents with an added layer of security and peace of mind, as they can always reach their children in case of emergencies. However, excessive screen time and the allure of online entertainment can create a divide between parents and children. It is crucial for parents to set healthy limits on screen time and actively engage with their children to build a strong bond based on trust and communication.

Privacy and Trust

Mobile phones bring forth new challenges in terms of privacy and trust within families. While it is important to respect each family member's privacy, the excessive use of mobile phones can lead to secrecy and mistrust. Parents may feel the need to monitor their children's online activities, which can strain the parent-child relationship. Building trust and open lines of communication are essential to address concerns and establish a balance between privacy and responsibility.

Fostering Healthy Habits

To ensure that mobile phones do not strain family bonds, it is essential to foster healthy habits and promote responsible phone usage. Setting limits on screen time, designating phone-free zones or hours, and encouraging face-to-face interactions can help maintain a healthy balance between virtual and real-life connections. It is important for parents to lead by example and establish healthy phone habits themselves, as children often emulate their parents' behaviors.

Conclusion

Mobile phones have undoubtedly transformed the way families communicate and stay connected. While they offer unprecedented convenience and opportunities for bridging gaps, they can also strain family dynamics if not used thoughtfully. It is crucial for families to recognize the potential impact of mobile phones on their relationships and take proactive steps to foster healthy habits and open lines of communication. By striking a balance between virtual connectivity and real-life connections, families can ensure that mobile phones strengthen rather than strain their bonds.

Chapter 8. Love and Romance in the Digital Era
Dating Apps and Relationship Formation

Introduction

The digital era has transformed various aspects of human life, including how we form romantic relationships. With the advent of mobile phones and dating apps, the landscape of love and romance has undergone significant changes. This article explores the impact of dating apps on relationship formation in the digital age, shedding light on the benefits and challenges they present.

The Rise of Dating Apps

Dating apps have emerged as a popular avenue for meeting potential partners in the digital era. With the convenience of mobile phones, people now have access to a vast pool of potential matches right at their fingertips. The rise of dating apps such as Tinder, Bumble, and OkCupid has revolutionized the way people connect and initiate romantic relationships.

Widening the Horizon

One of the significant advantages of dating apps is the ability to expand one's social circle and connect with individuals outside of traditional social circles. These apps provide a platform for meeting like-minded people, leading to increased chances of finding compatible partners. By breaking down geographical barriers, dating apps offer the opportunity to connect with individuals from different backgrounds and cultures.

Enhanced Accessibility

Dating apps have made the process of finding love more accessible to individuals with busy schedules or limited social circles. With a simple swipe or tap, users can explore numerous profiles and engage in conversations without the constraints of time and location. This accessibility has empowered people who may have previously struggled to meet potential partners, leading to increased inclusivity in the dating landscape.

Changing Communication Dynamics

The digital era has also influenced the way people communicate and interact within relationships. Dating apps often facilitate initial conversations through text-based messaging before transitioning to face-to-face meetings. This shift allows individuals to establish a connection based on personality and shared interests before physical appearances come into play. Consequently, dating apps have the potential to foster deeper emotional connections from the outset.

Overcoming Stigma

While dating apps have gained popularity, they have also faced criticism and stigma. However, as society becomes more accepting of digital platforms for relationship formation, this stigma is gradually diminishing. The ubiquity of dating apps has normalized their usage, making them a socially acceptable means of meeting potential partners. This normalization has helped individuals feel more comfortable using dating apps and embracing the possibilities they offer.

Challenges and Concerns

Despite the benefits, dating apps also pose challenges and concerns. One of the primary concerns is the tendency for superficial judgments based on appearance alone. The emphasis on profile pictures and brief bios can lead to snap judgments and shallow interactions. Additionally, the abundance of choices can lead to a paradox of choice, making it challenging to commit to one person. This can result in a "grass is greener" mentality, where individuals are constantly searching for the next best option.

Balancing Authenticity and Privacy

Another challenge is striking a balance between authenticity and privacy. While dating apps provide a platform to showcase oneself, there is also the risk of misrepresentation. People may curate their profiles to present an idealized version of themselves, potentially leading to disappointment when meeting in person. Additionally, concerns around privacy and data security have arisen, as users share personal information on these platforms.

Navigating Relationships in the Digital Age

The digital era has introduced new dynamics to relationships, challenging traditional norms and expectations. Couples must navigate issues such as defining boundaries regarding the usage of dating apps, dealing with jealousy arising from online interactions, and managing the impact of technology on intimacy. Building trust and effective communication become crucial in overcoming these challenges.

The Future of Love and Romance

As technology continues to evolve, so will the landscape of love and romance. Artificial intelligence and machine learning algorithms are already being utilized to enhance matching algorithms and provide personalized recommendations. Virtual reality and augmented reality technologies may also play a role in shaping the future of dating, enabling individuals to have immersive virtual experiences together.

Conclusion

Dating apps have undeniably transformed the way we form relationships in the digital era. They offer convenience, accessibility, and the opportunity to connect with a diverse range of individuals. However, they also bring challenges such as superficial judgments, paradox of choice, and privacy concerns. Navigating relationships in the digital age requires open communication, trust, and an understanding of the impact of technology. As we move forward, it is essential to strike a balance between the benefits and challenges of dating apps to foster meaningful and fulfilling relationships in the digital era.

Chapter 9. Cyberbullying and Online Harassment
Exploring the Dark Side of Connectivity

Introduction

In today's digital age, where mobile phones have become an integral part of our lives, connectivity has reached unprecedented levels. While this connectivity has brought numerous benefits and opportunities, it has also given rise to a dark side: cyberbullying and online harassment. These digital phenomena have become significant social issues, impacting individuals of all ages, genders, and backgrounds. This article delves into the world of cyberbullying and online harassment, highlighting their destructive effects and urging society to address and combat these challenges.

Understanding Cyberbullying

1. Defining Cyberbullying: Cyberbullying refers to the act of using digital platforms to deliberately intimidate, harass, or humiliate others. It involves repetitive, hostile behavior that targets individuals and takes advantage of the anonymity and distance provided by online platforms.

2. Forms of Cyberbullying: Cyberbullying manifests in various forms, including verbal abuse, spreading rumors, public shaming, sharing private information without consent, and creating fake profiles to deceive or harm others.

3. Impact on Victims: Cyberbullying can have severe consequences for victims, leading to emotional distress,

anxiety, depression, decreased self-esteem, and, in extreme cases, suicidal thoughts or actions. The 24/7 nature of online communication intensifies the trauma experienced by victims, making escape difficult.

Online Harassment

1. Defining Online Harassment: **Online harassment** encompasses a broader range of abusive behaviors that occur on digital platforms, such as social media, messaging apps, forums, and online gaming communities. It involves persistent and unwanted actions that cause fear, distress, or harm to individuals.

2. Types of Online Harassment: **Online harassment takes** many forms, including stalking, threats, sexual harassment, doxxing (revealing private information online), hate speech, and targeted campaigns to discredit or ruin someone's reputation.

3. Psychological and Emotional Toll: **Victims of online** harassment often experience heightened anxiety, fear, and paranoia due to the constant intrusion into their personal lives. The fear of being attacked or humiliated online can lead to self-censorship and withdrawal from online platforms, limiting social interactions.

The Role of Mobile Phones

1. Amplifying the Reach: Mobile phones play a pivotal role in the escalation of cyberbullying and online harassment. With easy access to the internet, social media apps, and instant messaging platforms, perpetrators can quickly target and torment their victims, regardless of geographical boundaries.

2. Anonymity and Impersonal Communication: Mobile phones provide a sense of anonymity, allowing bullies and harassers to hide behind screen names or create fake accounts, increasing their confidence to engage in harmful behaviors.

3. Perpetuation of Harm: The viral nature of mobile technology exacerbates the impact of cyberbullying and online harassment. Hurtful messages, images, or videos can spread rapidly, reaching a vast audience within minutes, inflicting long-lasting damage to the victim's reputation and well-being.

Psychological Factors

1. Deindividuation: The anonymity and detachment provided by mobile phones contribute to deindividuation, where individuals feel less accountable for their actions, leading to more aggressive and hurtful behavior.

2. Lack of Empathy: Online interactions often lack the non-verbal cues present in face-to-face communication, hindering empathy and increasing the likelihood of callous online behavior.

3. Digital Disinhibition Effect: The online environment fosters a sense of detachment from the consequences of one's actions, leading individuals to exhibit behavior they would not typically engage in offline.

Combating Cyberbullying and Online Harassment

1. Education and Awareness: Promoting digital literacy and raising awareness about the consequences of cyberbullying and online harassment are crucial in combating these issues. By educating individuals about responsible online

behavior, empathy, and the importance of standing up against harassment, we can foster a more compassionate digital society.

2. Stricter Regulations and Enforcement: Governments and online platforms must implement robust policies and regulations to address cyberbullying and online harassment effectively. This includes clear guidelines on reporting and handling incidents, as well as enforcing consequences for offenders.

3. Empowering Bystanders: Encouraging bystanders to intervene and support victims can make a significant difference. Empowering individuals to speak up against cyberbullying and online harassment helps create a culture of accountability and solidarity.

4. Mental Health Support: Providing accessible mental health resources and counseling services is essential for victims of cyberbullying and online harassment. Timely intervention and support can help alleviate the emotional and psychological impact of these experiences.

Conclusion

The rise of cyberbullying and online harassment in the digital age presents a complex challenge for our interconnected society. It is vital that we acknowledge and address these issues, working together to create safer digital spaces. By promoting empathy, digital literacy, and stricter regulations, we can foster a culture of respect and empathy, mitigating the destructive effects of cyberbullying and online harassment. It is our collective responsibility to ensure that connectivity and technological advancements do not come at the cost of human well-being and dignity in the digital realm.

Introduction

In today's digital age, mobile technology has become an integral part of our lives. From smartphones to wearable devices, we are constantly connected and reliant on these gadgets for communication, information access, and various day-to-day activities. However, the convenience and advantages offered by mobile technology come with a tradeoff—privacy concerns and the risk of surveillance. This article explores the delicate balance between the risks and rewards of mobile technology and the importance of safeguarding our privacy in an increasingly connected world.

The Rise of Mobile Technology

The advent of mobile technology has revolutionized the way we live and interact with the world. Smartphones have transformed into pocket-sized computers, providing us with a myriad of capabilities at our fingertips. From instant messaging and social media to online shopping and banking, mobile devices have made our lives more convenient and efficient.

Privacy in the Digital Era

As mobile technology continues to advance, the collection and storage of personal data have become pervasive. Our devices capture vast amounts of information about us, including our location, browsing habits, contacts, and even our biometric data. This data is often used by service providers and advertisers to personalize experiences and offer tailored recommendations. However, the very existence of this data poses significant privacy concerns.

The Risks of Surveillance

While surveillance can be used for legitimate purposes such as public safety and crime prevention, it also has the potential for abuse. Governments, corporations, and malicious actors can exploit the data collected through mobile technology to invade our privacy, track our movements, and monitor our online activities. This surveillance can infringe upon our fundamental rights and freedoms, eroding the trust we place in these technologies.

Personal Data Protection

To address the risks associated with privacy and surveillance, it is crucial to establish robust mechanisms for personal data protection. Governments and regulatory bodies must enforce strict privacy laws that define how personal information can be collected, stored, and used. Companies should adopt transparent practices and obtain informed consent before collecting and sharing user data. Additionally, individuals should take proactive steps to safeguard their privacy by using encryption tools, limiting data sharing, and being mindful of the apps they install on their devices.

Balancing Privacy and Convenience

While privacy is undoubtedly important, it is also essential to recognize the benefits that mobile technology brings to our lives. It allows us to stay connected with loved ones, access information on the go, and perform various tasks with ease. Achieving a balance between privacy and convenience is crucial, as overly stringent privacy measures may hinder innovation and technological advancements. Striking the right balance requires thoughtful consideration and collaboration among stakeholders.

Ethical Use of Surveillance

Surveillance technologies should be subject to ethical guidelines to prevent misuse and protect individual rights. Governments should ensure that surveillance activities are carried out within the bounds of the law, with appropriate oversight and accountability mechanisms in place. Transparency and public debate surrounding surveillance practices are essential to maintain trust and ensure that these tools are not used for unauthorized purposes.

Educating Users on Privacy

To empower individuals to protect their privacy, there is a need for comprehensive education on digital privacy and security. Users should be aware of the risks associated with mobile technology and understand the steps they can take to safeguard their personal information. Governments, schools, and organizations should invest in initiatives to raise awareness about privacy issues and provide practical guidance on privacy best practices.

Conclusion

Mobile technology has undoubtedly transformed our lives, but it has also given rise to concerns about privacy and surveillance. Striking a balance between the rewards of mobile technology and the risks it poses to our privacy is crucial. Governments, companies, and individuals must work together to protect personal data, ensure ethical surveillance practices, and educate users on privacy. Only through collective efforts can we harness the benefits of mobile technology while safeguarding our fundamental rights in the digital era.

Introduction

In today's digital era, mobile phones have become an integral part of our lives. These pocket-sized devices provide us with instant communication, access to information, and a plethora of entertainment options. However, the constant connectivity that mobile phones offer can have a significant impact on our mental health. In this article, we will explore the various ways in which mobile phones affect our psychological well-being and discuss strategies to maintain a healthy relationship with these devices.

The Addiction to Notifications

One of the primary reasons why mobile phones affect our mental health is the addiction to notifications. The constant buzzing and ringing of our phones create a sense of urgency and can lead to anxiety and stress. Research suggests that frequent exposure to notifications can disrupt our ability to focus, resulting in decreased productivity and increased feelings of overwhelm. It is crucial to recognize the addictive nature of notifications and take measures to manage them effectively.

Sleep Disturbances

The blue light emitted by mobile phone screens can interfere with our sleep patterns. The artificial light suppresses the production of melatonin, a hormone that regulates sleep, making it harder to fall asleep and maintain a restful sleep throughout the night. The excessive use of mobile phones, particularly before bedtime, has been linked to sleep disturbances, such as insomnia. Establishing a phone-free bedtime routine and avoiding screen time at least an hour before sleep can help improve sleep quality.

Social Comparison and FOMO

Mobile phones provide us with a constant stream of social media updates, which can lead to social comparison and the fear of missing out (FOMO). We often compare our lives to the carefully curated highlight reels of others, which can negatively impact our self-esteem and mental well-being. Moreover, the fear of missing out on social events or experiences depicted on social media can induce feelings of loneliness and inadequacy. Setting boundaries for social media usage and practicing mindfulness can help mitigate the negative effects of social comparison and FOMO.

Increased Stress and Anxiety

The constant connectivity of mobile phones can contribute to increased stress and anxiety levels. The expectation of being reachable at all times, coupled with the pressure to respond promptly, can lead to a heightened sense of stress. Additionally, the constant exposure to distressing news and information through social media and news applications can further exacerbate anxiety. Creating designated phone-free periods throughout the day and engaging in stress-reducing activities, such as exercise and meditation, can help manage stress and anxiety.

Impacts on Interpersonal Relationships

While mobile phones facilitate communication, they can also hinder the quality of our interpersonal relationships. Excessive phone use during social interactions can lead to decreased face-to-face engagement and a lack of presence. The constant distractions from notifications and social media can prevent meaningful connections and impair the development of empathy and understanding. It is essential to prioritize in-person interactions and establish phone-free zones during social gatherings to nurture healthy relationships.

Digital Detox and Mindful Phone Usage

To maintain a healthy relationship with our mobile phones and protect our mental health, it is crucial to practice digital detoxes and mindful phone usage. A digital detox involves taking a break from mobile phones and other digital devices for a specified period. It allows us to disconnect, recharge, and recalibrate our relationship with technology. Mindful phone usage, on the other hand, involves being aware of our phone habits and consciously setting boundaries to ensure that our phone use aligns with our well-being goals.

Conclusion

Mobile phones have undoubtedly revolutionized the way we communicate and access information. However, the constant connectivity they offer can have detrimental effects on our mental health. It is essential to be aware of the potential negative impacts and take proactive steps to manage our relationship with mobile phones. By practicing mindful phone usage, setting boundaries, and prioritizing real-life connections, we can strike a balance between the benefits of technology and our mental well-being. Remember, our mental health should always be a priority in this digital age.

Chapter 12. Education and Learning
Mobile Phones as Tools for Knowledge Access

Introduction

In recent years, mobile phones have become an integral part of our daily lives. These portable devices have revolutionized communication and entertainment, but their impact extends far beyond these areas. Mobile phones are increasingly being recognized as powerful tools for accessing knowledge and enhancing education. With their widespread availability and ever-increasing capabilities, mobile phones have the potential to bridge the gap in educational access and transform the way we learn. In this article, we will explore the various ways in which mobile phones can be used as tools for knowledge access and their impact on education.

Access to Information

Mobile phones provide easy and instant access to a vast amount of information. With internet connectivity and search engines at our fingertips, we can access knowledge on any topic with just a few taps. This accessibility is especially valuable for students who may not have access to traditional libraries or educational resources. Mobile phones enable them to explore a wide range of subjects, conduct research, and access educational materials, including e-books, academic journals, and online courses.

Interactive Learning

Mobile phones offer numerous opportunities for interactive learning. Educational apps and platforms provide interactive quizzes, games, and simulations that make learning engaging and enjoyable. These apps cater to different learning styles and allow students to learn at their own pace. Through mobile phones, students can participate in virtual classrooms, join online discussion forums, and collaborate with peers on educational projects. The interactive nature of mobile learning encourages active participation, critical thinking, and problem-solving skills.

Personalized Learning

Mobile phones enable personalized learning experiences tailored to individual needs and preferences. Educational apps and platforms often use adaptive learning algorithms to assess a student's strengths and weaknesses and provide personalized recommendations. This personalized approach helps students focus on areas where they need improvement, making their learning journey more efficient and effective. Moreover, mobile phones allow students to set their own learning goals, track their progress, and receive timely feedback, empowering them to take ownership of their education.

Language Learning

Mobile phones can be powerful tools for language learning. Language learning apps offer interactive lessons, vocabulary drills, and pronunciation practice, allowing learners to develop their language skills anytime and anywhere. Mobile phones also facilitate language immersion through audio and video resources, enabling learners to listen to authentic conversations and watch foreign-language films. Additionally, language translation apps help students understand and communicate in different languages, breaking down language barriers and fostering global communication.

Bridging the Digital Divide

The digital divide refers to the gap between those who have access to digital technologies and those who do not. Mobile phones, with their affordability and widespread availability, have the potential to bridge this divide. In many developing countries, where access to traditional educational resources is limited, mobile phones offer a lifeline for learning. Students can access educational content, connect with teachers and fellow learners, and participate in online courses even in areas with limited infrastructure. Mobile phones empower disadvantaged communities to overcome barriers to education and acquire the knowledge they need to thrive.

Skills Development

Mobile phones facilitate the development of various skills that are crucial for success in the digital age. Digital literacy, including the ability to navigate online resources, evaluate information critically, and protect one's digital identity, is increasingly important. Mobile phones provide a platform for students to develop these skills naturally as they interact with digital content. Moreover, mobile phones can support the development of creativity, problem-solving, and digital communication skills through educational apps and tools designed for these purposes.

Conclusion

Mobile phones have emerged as powerful tools for knowledge access and learning. Their accessibility, interactive nature, and personalized approach make them valuable assets in education. With mobile phones, students can access a wealth of information, engage in interactive and personalized learning experiences, bridge the digital divide, and develop essential digital skills. However, it is important to ensure responsible and mindful use of mobile phones in educational settings. Educators, policymakers, and parents should collaborate to harness the potential of mobile phones and integrate them effectively into formal and informal learning environments. By leveraging mobile technology, we can create a future where education is accessible to all, regardless of geographical or socioeconomic barriers.

Chapter 13. Work-Life Balance in the Digital Age
Mobile Phones and Professional Boundaries

Introduction

In today's digital age, where mobile phones have become an integral part of our lives, achieving a healthy work-life balance has become increasingly challenging. The boundaries between work and personal life have blurred, leading to constant connectivity and an always-on mentality. This article explores the impact of mobile phones on work-life balance and discusses strategies for establishing and maintaining professional boundaries in the digital era.

The Blurring Boundaries

Mobile phones have revolutionized the way we work, enabling us to stay connected and productive regardless of time and location. While this connectivity brings numerous benefits, it has also eroded the boundaries between work and personal life. With work emails, messages, and notifications flooding our devices, it has become difficult to switch off and disconnect from work obligations. As a result, many individuals find it challenging to create a clear distinction between their professional and personal lives.

The Negative Consequences

The lack of work-life balance can have detrimental effects on individuals' well-being, productivity, and relationships. Constant exposure to work-related communication through mobile phones can lead to increased stress levels, burnout, and a decline in mental health. Moreover, the blurring of boundaries can strain personal relationships and impede the ability to fully engage in non-work activities. It is crucial to address these negative consequences and find ways to establish healthier boundaries in the digital age.

Establishing Professional Boundaries

To achieve a better work-life balance, it is important to set clear professional boundaries. Here are some strategies that can help individuals regain control over their time and establish healthier boundaries in the digital era:

1. Define Work Hours

Set specific work hours and communicate them clearly with colleagues and clients. By establishing designated times for work, you create a structure that allows you to allocate time for personal activities and minimize interruptions during non-work hours.

2. Turn off Push Notifications

Disable non-essential notifications on your mobile phone. Constant interruptions from emails, messages, and social media updates can disrupt your focus and invade your personal time. By turning off push notifications, you regain control over when and how you engage with work-related communication.

3. Create Physical Separation

Designate specific spaces for work and personal activities. If possible, have a separate workspace where you can concentrate on work tasks. Once you step away from that space, make a conscious effort to disconnect and engage in personal activities without the distractions of work-related matters.

4. Establish Digital Boundaries

Create rules for yourself regarding mobile phone usage. For instance, avoid checking work emails or messages during designated personal time. Instead, allocate specific times to attend to work-related matters and avoid constant monitoring of your phone.

5. Prioritize Self-Care

Make self-care a priority and allocate time for activities that promote relaxation, physical well-being, and personal growth. Engaging in hobbies, exercise, spending time with loved ones, and pursuing interests outside of work can help restore balance and improve overall well-being.

Maintaining Boundaries

Establishing boundaries is only the first step; it is equally important to maintain them consistently. Here are some tips for maintaining professional boundaries in the long run:

1. Communicate Expectations

Clearly communicate your boundaries to colleagues, clients, and supervisors. Educate them about your designated work hours and the importance of respecting your personal time. This open communication can help manage expectations and reduce the likelihood of work-related intrusions outside of designated work hours.

2. Lead by Example

If you are in a leadership position, it is crucial to set an example by respecting and encouraging work-life balance among your team members. Avoid sending work-related emails or messages during non-work hours, and promote a culture that values personal well-being and boundaries.

3. Practice Digital Detox

Periodically disconnect from digital devices altogether. Take short breaks or vacations where you limit your mobile phone usage and prioritize relaxation and rejuvenation. Detoxifying from constant connectivity can help you recharge and come back with renewed energy and focus.

4. Seek Support

If you find it challenging to maintain boundaries on your own, seek support from colleagues, friends, or family members. Share your struggles and goals with trusted individuals who can provide accountability and offer guidance in maintaining a healthy work-life balance.

Conclusion

In the digital age, where mobile phones dominate our professional and personal lives, establishing and maintaining work-life balance has become more crucial than ever. By setting clear boundaries, prioritizing personal time, and communicating expectations, individuals can regain control over their time and well-being. Remember, a healthy work-life balance not only benefits individuals but also enhances productivity, satisfaction, and overall quality of life.

Chapter 14. Civic Engagement and Activism
Mobile Phones as Tools for Social Change

Introduction

In today's digital age, mobile phones have become ubiquitous, serving as powerful tools that connect individuals across the globe. With their widespread accessibility and functionality, mobile phones have transformed the landscape of civic engagement and activism, empowering individuals to initiate and participate in social change movements. This article explores the ways in which mobile phones have revolutionized activism, fostering increased awareness, mobilization, and collective action among individuals and communities.

Mobilizing Awareness

Mobile phones have emerged as vital instruments for raising awareness about various social issues. Social media platforms and messaging apps have become virtual hubs for sharing news, information, and personal experiences. Through the simple act of sharing and forwarding messages, individuals can disseminate information rapidly and reach a wide audience. This real-time information exchange promotes knowledge dissemination and enables individuals to stay informed about pressing social concerns.

Grassroots Organizing

Mobile phones have proven to be invaluable tools for grassroots organizing. Activists can utilize social media platforms, such as Facebook and Twitter, to create online communities and organize events, rallies, and protests. These platforms serve as virtual meeting spaces, allowing like-minded individuals to connect, share ideas, and plan collective actions. By leveraging the power of mobile phones, activists can quickly mobilize a large number of supporters, amplifying their voices and increasing their impact.

Citizen Journalism

Mobile phones have empowered ordinary citizens to become citizen journalists, documenting and sharing real-time information about social injustices and human rights violations. The ubiquity of smartphones equipped with high-quality cameras enables individuals to capture and disseminate evidence of wrongdoing. Citizen journalists can bypass traditional media gatekeepers, sharing their footage and stories directly with the public via social media platforms, generating awareness and spurring action.

Fundraising and Donations

Mobile phones have facilitated the democratization of fundraising and donations, enabling individuals to contribute to social causes directly from their devices. With the emergence of mobile payment systems and crowdfunding platforms, supporters can make financial contributions with a few taps on their screens. This ease of donating has lowered barriers to entry, allowing individuals to contribute even small amounts that, when pooled together, can make a significant impact on grassroots initiatives and charitable organizations.

Global Solidarity

Mobile phones have played a crucial role in fostering global solidarity among activists and individuals working towards social change. Social media platforms have facilitated cross-border connections, enabling activists from different parts of the world to share their experiences, strategies, and successes. This exchange of ideas and support has led to the formation of transnational movements, uniting people across borders to address shared challenges, such as climate change, human rights, and inequality.

Monitoring and Accountability

Mobile phones have become powerful tools for monitoring and holding authorities accountable. Through the use of live streaming and video recording, individuals can document instances of police brutality, corruption, and other abuses of power. These recordings serve as crucial evidence and catalysts for justice, compelling action from both local and international communities. The ability to capture and share incidents in real-time has shifted the balance of power, making it more challenging for injustices to go unnoticed or unaddressed.

Conclusion

Mobile phones have emerged as transformative tools for civic engagement and activism, revolutionizing the way individuals participate in social change movements. From mobilizing awareness and grassroots organizing to citizen journalism and global solidarity, mobile phones have democratized activism, giving a voice to marginalized communities and enabling individuals to become agents of change. As technology continues to evolve, it is crucial to harness the power of mobile phones responsibly and ethically, ensuring their continued impact in shaping a more just and equitable world.

Introduction

In today's digital era, mobile phones have become an integral part of our lives. They have revolutionized communication and transformed the way we interact with the world around us. While these devices offer numerous benefits, they have also given rise to a generation gap in terms of technology usage. This article explores the impact of mobile phones on intergenerational relationships and provides insights on how to bridge the gap.

The Generational Divide

The rapid advancement of mobile technology has resulted in varying levels of adoption across different age groups. Younger generations, such as Millennials (born from 1981 to 1996) and Gen Z (born from 1997 to 2012), have grown up with smartphones and are highly proficient in using them. On the other hand, older generations, such as Baby Boomers (born from 1946 to 1964) and Gen X (born from 1965 to 1980), may struggle to keep pace with the ever-evolving features and functionalities of mobile devices. This divide can create barriers to effective communication and understanding.

Communication Challenges

Mobile phones have revolutionized communication by providing instant connectivity and various channels to stay in touch. However, different generations may have contrasting preferences when it comes to communication styles. While younger individuals embrace texting, social media, and video calls, older individuals may still prefer traditional phone calls or face-to-face interactions. This disconnect in communication preferences can hinder meaningful exchanges and lead to misunderstandings.

Bridging the Gap

1. Mutual Learning: Intergenerational relationships can be enhanced through mutual learning and understanding. Younger individuals can help older generations navigate the world of mobile phones by offering patient guidance and support. Conversely, older individuals can share their wisdom and life experiences, fostering a sense of respect and appreciation.

2. Technology Literacy Programs: Community organizations and educational institutions can play a crucial role in bridging the generation gap by offering technology literacy programs tailored to older adults. These programs can provide hands-on training, address specific challenges faced by older individuals, and boost their confidence in using mobile devices.

3. Regular Communication: To bridge the gap, regular communication is essential. Encouraging regular interactions, whether through phone calls, video chats, or social media platforms, can help build familiarity and strengthen intergenerational bonds. It is important to find a balance between the preferred communication methods of both generations.

Fostering Empathy and Patience

Both younger and older individuals need to cultivate empathy and patience to foster better intergenerational relationships in the digital age. Younger generations should understand that not everyone is as tech-savvy as they are and that the learning curve may be steeper for older individuals. Conversely, older generations should appreciate the benefits of technology and make efforts to adapt to its usage.

The Importance of Boundaries

While it is crucial to bridge the generation gap, it is equally important to establish boundaries and respect individual preferences. Mobile phones should not overshadow face-to-face interactions or quality time spent with loved ones. Setting designated "tech-free" times or creating tech-free zones can help strike a balance between the digital world and real-life connections.

Conclusion

Mobile phones have undeniably transformed the way we communicate and connect with one another. However, they have also given rise to a generation gap, posing challenges to intergenerational relationships. By fostering mutual learning, offering technology literacy programs, promoting regular communication, cultivating empathy and patience, and establishing boundaries, we can navigate the generation gap and strengthen intergenerational relationships in the digital age. By bridging this gap, we can create a harmonious coexistence between different generations, benefiting from the wisdom of the past and the possibilities of the future.

Chapter 16. The Future of Mobile Technology
Anticipating Social Shifts in a Connected World

Introduction

Mobile technology has transformed the way we live, work, and interact with the world around us. From the advent of smartphones to the rise of mobile applications, our reliance on mobile devices continues to grow. As we look to the future, it is crucial to anticipate the social shifts that will accompany further advancements in mobile technology. This article explores the potential changes we may witness and their implications for individuals and society as a whole.

Enhanced Connectivity and Communication

In a connected world, mobile technology will foster even greater connectivity and communication. The advent of 5G (launched in 2019) and 6G (likely to launch in 2030) networks will enable lightning-fast data transmission, allowing for seamless video conferencing, real-time collaboration, and enhanced virtual experiences. This increased connectivity will bridge geographical divides, enabling people to connect and collaborate across borders. However, it also raises concerns about privacy and data security, as more personal information is shared online.

The Rise of Augmented Reality (AR) and Virtual Reality (VR)

Mobile technology is set to revolutionize our perception of reality through the widespread adoption of augmented reality (AR) and virtual reality (VR). AR overlays digital information onto the real world, while VR immerses users in simulated environments. These technologies will revolutionize various industries, such as gaming, education, healthcare, and even retail. They will redefine the way we experience entertainment, learn new skills, and make purchasing decisions.

The Internet of Things (IoT) and Smart Cities

Mobile technology will play a crucial role in the development of smart cities, where various devices and systems are interconnected through the Internet of Things (IoT). With mobile devices acting as the gateway to this interconnected network, individuals will have more control over their living spaces, from managing energy consumption to optimizing transportation. However, this increased reliance on technology raises concerns about cybersecurity and data privacy, requiring robust safeguards.

Mobile Healthcare and Telemedicine

The future of mobile technology holds tremendous potential for healthcare. Mobile devices will enable personalized healthcare solutions, such as wearable health trackers, remote patient monitoring, and telemedicine. Patients will have access to real-time health data, allowing for early detection and preventive care. Telemedicine will enable remote consultations and improve access to healthcare in remote areas. However, challenges such as data security and regulatory frameworks need to be addressed for widespread adoption.

Workforce Mobility and Remote Collaboration

Mobile technology has already facilitated remote work to a great extent, and its future advancements will further enable workforce mobility and remote collaboration. With mobile devices acting as powerful productivity tools, individuals will have the freedom to work from anywhere. This will lead to a more flexible work-life balance, reduced commute times, and increased job opportunities for those in remote areas. However, it may also blur the boundaries between work and personal life, necessitating effective time management and setting boundaries.

Ethical and Societal Implications

As we embrace the future of mobile technology, we must also address the ethical and societal implications that arise. Issues such as digital addiction, privacy concerns, and the digital divide need to be carefully considered. Striking a balance between connectivity and personal well-being is crucial. Additionally, efforts should be made to bridge the digital divide, ensuring that everyone has equal access to mobile technology and its benefits.

Conclusion

The future of mobile technology holds immense potential for transforming various aspects of our lives. Enhanced connectivity, augmented reality, smart cities, mobile healthcare, remote work, and the ethical implications that accompany these advancements will shape our society in profound ways. As we navigate this evolving landscape, it is crucial to anticipate and address the social shifts that arise, ensuring that the benefits of mobile technology are accessible to all while safeguarding individual privacy and well-being. By embracing the opportunities and addressing the challenges, we can shape a future where mobile technology enhances our lives and fosters a more connected and inclusive world.

"Social Impact of Mobile Phones in the Digital Age" is a thought-provoking exploration of the profound influence that mobile phones have had on our society. This book delves into the various aspects of the social consequences brought about by the mobile revolution. From the transformation of communication methods to the redefinition of relationships in the digital era, each chapter provides a comprehensive analysis of the impact of mobile phones on different facets of our lives. It examines the breaking of geographical barriers, the rise of social media, the shaping of identity, the power of online platforms for community building, the dynamics of family bonds, the complexities of love and romance in the digital era, the dark side of connectivity including cyberbullying and online harassment, the delicate balance between privacy and surveillance, the implications for mental health, the role of mobile phones in education and learning, the challenges of work-life balance, the potential for civic engagement and activism, the intergenerational relationships shaped by mobile technology, and offers a glimpse into the future of mobile technology and its anticipated social shifts in an increasingly connected world. This book is a must-read for anyone interested in understanding the complex interplay between mobile phones and society in the digital age.

ABOUT THE AUTHOR

Mr. C. P. Kumar is a retired Scientist 'G' from National Institute of Hydrology, Roorkee, Uttarakhand, India. He is also a Reiki Healer and Chakra Balancing practitioner (with pendulum dowsing) and offers Emotional Freedom Technique (EFT) to help individuals with emotional issues. Mr. Kumar has authored many books on technical, spiritual, and social topics.

For further details, you may visit his webpage
https://www.angelfire.com/nh/cpkumar/virgo.html